MW01031989

Too Tall, Too Small

Luke 19:1–10
(Zacchaeus)

by Mary Manz Simon
Illustrated by Dennis Jones

CPH™
SAINT LOUIS

Books by Mary Manz Simon

Hear Me Read Level 1

What Next? CPH
Drip Drop, CPH
Jibber Jabber, CPH
Hide the Baby, CPH
Toot! Toot! CPH
Bing! CPH
Whoops! CPH
Send a Baby, CPH
A Silent Night, CPH
Follow That Star, CPH
Row the Boat, CPH
Rumble, Rumble, CPH
Who Will Help? CPH
Sit Down, CPH
Come to Jesus, CPH
Too Tall, Too Small, CPH
Hurry, Hurry! CPH
Where Is Jesus? CPH

Hear Me Read Level 2

The No-Go King, CPH
Hurray for the Lord's Army! CPH
The Hide-and-Seek Prince, CPH
Daniel and the Tattletales, CPH
The First Christmas, CPH
Through the Roof, CPH
A Walk on the Waves, CPH
Thank You, Jesus, CPH

God's Children Pray, CPH
My First Diary, CPH
52 Ways to Raise Happy, Loving Kids
  Thomas Nelson Publishing

Little Visits on the Go, CPH
Little Visits 1-2-3, CPH
Little Visits with Jesus, CPH
More Little Visits with Jesus, CPH

Copyright © 1990 Concordia Publishing House
3558 S. Jefferson Avenue, St. Louis, MO 63118-3968
Manufactured in the United States of America

Library of Congress Cataloging-in-Publication Data

Simon, Mary Manz, 1948–
    Too tall, too small: Luke 19:1–10 : Zacchaeus / by Mary Manz Simon.
    p.   cm. — (Hear me read Bible stories)
    Summary: Retells for beginning readers the Bible story of Zacchaeus and his efforts to see Jesus in the crowd.
    ISBN 0–570–041856–6
    1. Zacchaeus (Biblical character)—Juvenile literature. 2. Bible Stories, English—N.T.Luke. [1. Zacchaeus (Biblical character) 2. Bible stories—N.T.] I. Title. II. Title: Zacchaeus. III. Series: Simon, Mary Manz, 1948–   Hear me read Bible stories.
BS2520. Z3S56 1990   89-35447
226.4'09505—dc20   CIP
                                    AC

2 3 4 5 6 7 8 9 10   00 99 98 97 96 95 94

Name
_____

Date
_____

Presented by
_____

To the Adult:

Early readers need two kinds of reading: they need to be read to, and they need to do their own reading. The Hear Me Read Bible Stories series helps you to encourage your child with both kinds.

For example, your child might read this book as you sit together. Listen attentively. Assist gently, if needed. Encourage, be patient, and be positive about your child's efforts.

Then perhaps you'd like to share this Bible story in an easy-to-understand translation or paraphrase.

Using both types of reading gives your child a chance to develop new skills and pride in reading. You share and support your child's excitement.

As a mother and a teacher, I anticipate the joy your child will feel in saying, "Hear me read Bible stories!"

Mary Manz Simon

For Christina Marie Simon
Psalm 23

See the people.

The people want to see Jesus.

"I want to see Jesus,"

said Zacchaeus.

"I want to see Jesus, too."

"The people are too tall,"

said Zacchaeus.

"I am too small."

"I will climb up, up to see,"

said Zacchaeus.

"Jesus will be close to me."

"The people are too tall.

The animals are too tall.

I am too small,"

said Zacchaeus.

"I will climb up, up to see,"

said Zacchaeus.

"Jesus will be close to me."

See the people.

See the animals.

See Zacchaeus.

"The people are too tall.

The animals are too tall.

The trees are too tall.

I am too small," said Zacchaeus.

"I want to see Jesus.

I want to see Jesus, too."

The people are tall.

The animals are tall.

The trees are tall.

"The trees are tall,"

said Zacchaeus.

"Wow!"

"I will climb the trees,"

said Zacchaeus.

"I will climb the tall, tall trees."

"I will climb up, up to see,"

said Zacchaeus.

"Jesus will be close to me."

"I see Jesus.

I see Jesus come.

Jesus will see me,"

said Zacchaeus.

"Zacchaeus," said Jesus.

"Zacchaeus, come see Me.

Come close to Me."

"Wow!" said Zacchaeus.

About the Author

Mary Manz Simon holds a doctoral degree in education with a specialty in early childhood education. She has taught at levels from preschool through postgraduate. Dr. Simon has also authored the newly released *God's Children Pray* and the best-selling *Little Visits with Jesus* and *More Little Visits with Jesus*. She and her husband, the Reverend Henry A. Simon, are the parents of three children.